MINDFULNESS IN EVERYDAY LIFE

100 SMALL & EFFICIENT MINDFULNESS EXERCISES FOR IN BETWEEN

CONTENTS-
DIRECTORY

 GOOD MORNING! — 1 - 10

 MORNING ROUTINES — 11 - 20

 HAVE BREAKFAST — 21 - 30

 WORK/SCHOOL/STUDY — 31 - 40

 LUNCH BREAK — 41 - 50

 FREE TIME ACTIVITIES — 51 - 60

 HOUSEHOLD TASKS — 61 - 70

 DINNER — 71 - 80

 RECREATION — 81 - 90

 GOOD NIGHT! — 91 - 100

Foreword

Welcome to this book, which summarizes 100 small and efficient mindfulness exercises for everyday life.

In an increasingly hectic world, many of us are looking for ways to bring more calm, clarity and contentment into our lives. Mindfulness offers a wonderful way to cultivate these qualities.

Mindfulness can be defined as a state in which we remain in the present moment consciously and non-judgmentally. It means focusing our attention on the here and now and observing our thoughts, feelings and sensations with openness and acceptance.

The benefits of mindfulness are numerous and scientifically well-documented. Regular mindfulness practice can help reduce stress, improve concentration, promote emotional stability and increase general well-being. It can help us deal with the challenges of everyday life in a more calm and balanced way.

This book is especially intended for people who want to get into the topic of mindfulness.

The 100 exercises in this book are deliberately kept short and can be easily integrated into everyday life. Each exercise can be done in just a few minutes, so you don't have to plan a lot of time. Just a few minutes a day can be enough to feel the positive effects of mindfulness.

To facilitate the integration of mindfulness into your daily life, certain anchor points can be helpful. These anchor points can be everyday events such as the alarm clock going off, a call on your phone, or a car driving by. Each of these events can serve as a reminder to pause, take a breath, and re-center yourself.

Mindfulness is possible anywhere and at any time. With the exercises in this book, I want to show you that being mindful does not require great effort. Every moment offers the opportunity to practice mindfulness and thus bring more peace and clarity into your life.

I wish you much joy and success on your journey to more mindfulness and well-being in everyday life!

GOOD MORNING!

This chapter is entirely dedicated to mindfulness in the morning.

The beginning of the day is a precious moment to bring body and mind into harmony and lay the foundation for a mindful and fulfilling day.

**The following ten exercises have been carefully selected to gently guide you into the day.
They include breathing exercises, stretching exercises and techniques for muscle tension
and
-Relaxation.**

These exercises not only help you to reduce physical tension, but also promote mental clarity and inner peace.
Take your time to perform each exercise consciously and with full attention.
Let the instructions guide you and feel how mindfulness enriches your morning routine.

May this start to the day bring you well-being and energy.

Stretching to wake up

Do not get up immediately after waking up or when the alarm clock rings.

Use the time in bed and sit on the edge of the bed to stretch and extend yourself extensively.

Stretch your arms high above your head.
Rotate your upper body by turning it left and right.
Let your head move towards your chest and move your chin alternately from left to right towards your shoulders.

Stretching activates your muscles.

Breathe in and out deeply.

Enjoy the moment once again before you start your day.

1

Thoughtless

It is best to sit cross-legged in your bed or on a blanket on the floor.
Close your eyes and continue breathing at your own pace.

**Now count your breaths from 1 to 10.
Your task is simply to think about NOTHING when counting from 1-10.**

As you breathe in, you begin to count internally
"1"
and as you exhale you continue the count
"2".

Keep doing this until you reach 10.

Are you thinking about something in the meantime?
Then start counting again from "1".

Ear Massage

Sit in your bed or on the edge of it.

Now take your ears in your hands and rub them for about 30 seconds.

Rub your ears between your fingers in circular motions. Use the entire area between the earlobe and the shell.
Get faster and faster at this.

**Then feel into your ears.
How warm did they get?**

Can you feel the warmth throughout the rest of your body because it has spread?

The massage should also help you start the day more alert.

Focused breathing exercise

Sit up straight and close your eyes.
Breathe in deeply and then let your breath flow in a relaxed manner.

Now place your hands on top of each other on your stomach below your belly button.

Gently feel into your hands and observe how your belly moves beneath them with each breath.
Feel the light pressure of your hands on your stomach.

How does your stomach feel right now?
Is he tense or relaxed?

Try to become a little calmer and more relaxed with each breath. As soon as you have gathered enough strength and feel fit for the day, get up and start your day.

Recap

You can do this exercise in bed right after you wake up.
To do this, close your eyes again or fixate on a point in your surroundings.

Just think back to yesterday.

What happened yesterday?
Were there any happy moments that you like to remember?
What have you seen?
Are you angry about something?

If you are still having negative thoughts from the previous day, try to accept them.
Imagine the situation in a cloud and let a strong wind push it aside until you can see a cloudless and sunny sky.
Use happy moments to motivate yourself for today.

Slow morning routine

Today, try changing your morning routine and doing each task one at a time.

Multitasking and mindfulness do not mix well.

Today, try not to brush your teeth while checking your messages, choosing your outfit, and preparing your coffee maker. Do each step consciously and calmly before starting the next one.

If you don't have enough time for this, change your routine.
Do some tasks the night before or set your alarm earlier to have more time in the morning.
This way you can start the day calmly and refreshed.

Contagious friendliness

Start your morning with the intention of making the day as pleasant as possible.

Today, try to approach everyone you meet with helpfulness, cheerfulness and kindness.

Give your brightest smile to your family, friends, work colleagues and even strangers.

Do you feel the difference? Do you experience joy and helpfulness in response?

Just give it a try.

Interplay of the senses

Sit up straight.
Breathe in and out deeply.

Now consciously move back and forth between your senses.

Feel your breathing.
How does your breathing feel?
Look around consciously.
What can you see that you haven't noticed before?
Focus on what you hear.
Are there any sounds or noises that you notice?

Do the exercise a few times in a row and take 2-3 minutes.

Chest and abdominal breathing

After you wake up, feel free to lie down and relax and turn onto your back.

Place your right hand on your chest and your left hand on your stomach.

During the next 5 breaths, try to consciously breathe into your chest. Use your breathing to push your chest out towards your hand.

Next, breathe deeply into your stomach 5 times and push your left hand upwards.

Pay close attention to the movements.
Which breathing feels better for your body?

Feel free to repeat the alternate breathing over and over again within 2-3 minutes.

Lightning relaxation

As soon as you get up, you can do a short relaxation exercise.
To do this, stand with your feet hip-width apart.

Try to tense as many parts of your body as possible at the same time.

To do this, hold your breath for a moment.
Tighten all the muscles in your face and make a face.
Pull your shoulders toward your ears.
Tense your arms and clench your hands into fists.
Squeeze your glutes together.
Let your leg muscles freeze tightly.

Stay in this position for 5-7 seconds.
**Now relax all muscles at the same time and consciously breathe out strongly.
How do your muscles feel now?**
Feel free to repeat this 5 times in a row.

10

MORNING ROUTINES

Welcome to this chapter, which is dedicated to mindfulness during the morning preparation for the day.

This valuable time in the morning offers you the opportunity to consciously and mindfully prepare yourself for the day ahead.

The following ten exercises are carefully selected to help you stay present and alert during your daily morning routines such as showering, brushing your teeth and getting dressed.

The chapter includes breathing exercises, tactile exercises and attention exercises.

These mindfulness exercises will help you to fully experience the moment, reduce stress and create a positive mood for the day. Take the freedom to do each exercise with mindfulness and concentration.
Feel how your morning routine is enriched by these little islands of calm and attention.

Mindful showering

Start your day with a refreshing shower and take the time to experience it consciously.

Feel the water jet gliding gently over your skin.
Notice the different sensations – are some areas of your body more sensitive than others?

Occasionally vary the water temperature between warm and cold.
Observe how your body reacts to these temperature changes.

How does your skin feel when you apply shower gel or soap?
Does it tingle slightly?

Try to put your thoughts aside and concentrate on fully feeling and enjoying the shower experience.

Give yourself a smile

Stand in front of the mirror and observe your facial features mindfully.

**Now smile at yourself in the mirror.
Give yourself your most beautiful smile.**

Watch how your facial features change. Do your eyes smile as well?
How does smiling affect your mood?

Try to smile even more.

Now feel how the smile not only spreads across your face, but also how the emotions change in your body.

Send kindness to your heart for the day ahead.

Slow motion

Today, do one activity from your morning routine in slow motion.

For example, apply cream to your face slowly and consciously.
Perform each movement mindfully.
Circle your eyes and continue on your cheeks.
Gently feel into your fingertips and feel the contact with the face.

You can also do other activities such as brushing your teeth, shaving or combing your hair.
The main thing is that you perform the movements calmly and very slowly.

**How does the slower activity feel to you?
Does it give you a little relaxation for the moment?**

Facial tactile exercises

Do you actually know how your face feels?
Today, don't look in the mirror when you're in the
bathroom, but close your eyes.

Feel and explore your face with your fingertips.

Run your hand along your face.
Start at your forehead, move down your cheeks to
your chin.
How does the shape of your nose feel?
Move over your eyes, over your eyebrows and over
your temples to your ears.
Touch your lips.
How big and soft do they feel?

Can you feel what you look like?
Try to see with your hands.

14

Atmantra

Stand upright and relaxed.

Focus your attention on your breathing and let thoughts pass by calmly.

Now associate a calming sentence or words with your breath.
For example:

Inhale "relaxation", exhale "calm".

Repeat this for 2-3 minutes.

Mindfulness when dressing

Focus your attention on the sensory experiences while getting dressed.

**Pick up each item of clothing individually.
Feel the texture of the fabric between your fingers.**

Pay attention to how the material feels.
Is it soft, rough or smooth?

Take a close look at the colors and patterns of your clothes.
Look at the details you would normally overlook, like seams, buttons and prints.

As you put on each piece of clothing, notice the contact of the fabric with your skin.
Does it feel different on your body than in your hands?

Colors in your environment

You can do this meditation in your bathroom or any other place.
Open your eyes and observe your outside world mindfully and consciously.

Look at the colors of your surroundings **exactly on.**

Find the color green.

What green things can you see right now?
How many objects can you discover?
Do you suddenly notice things you didn't see before?

Use your entire environment to keep searching.

Inventory

Take a little time out and count the cosmetic products in your bathroom.
Now try to synchronize your breathing with the count.

1 - Inhale
2 - Exhale
3 - Inhale
4- Exhale

How many shampoo bottles, creams, toothpaste tubes, razors, shower gel bottles and brushes can you find?
Take 2 - 3 minutes for this process.
If the items are not enough, move on to other items or start again at the beginning.

Facial massage

Sit or stand in a relaxed position.
Now use your fingertips to massage and pat your face.

Start with circular movements on your forehead and work your way over your temples to your cheeks and down to your chin.

Now start again at your forehead and this time tap all areas up to your chin with your fingertips.

How does your face feel?

Repeat the process several times.

Mood check

Take a moment for a quick mood check.
Sit or stand quietly and keep your body completely still.
Turn your attention inward and pay attention to your feelings.

How do you feel at this moment?
How is your mood?

Become aware of your feelings by naming them objectively.

"I feel cheerful/well-rested/bad-tempered/tired/stressed/happy…"

Everyone experiences good days and not so good days.
All of this is fine and allowed.
Accept the feeling and embrace it without judging it.

HAVE BREAKFAST

This chapter invites you to accompany yourself with physical mindfulness during breakfast.

Here you will find ten exercises that will help you make breakfast a moment of calm and presence.

From short eating exercises to brief sensory perceptions to small slowdowns – these practices allow you to consciously feel your body and create moments of inner peace.

These mindfulness exercises will help you to consciously enjoy every bite, sharpen your senses and start the morning at a more relaxed pace.
Take the freedom to perform each exercise with full attention and dedication. Feel how your breakfast routine is enriched by these moments of mindfulness.

Coffee ceremony

Maybe you are one of those people who like to make a fresh coffee or tea in the morning.

Once your drink is ready, sit down at a table and take a short break.

**Now look at the drink.
Which color is it?
What is its composition and ingredients?
Where does it come from and what journey does it take to get to your cup?**

Take a moment to notice your thoughts about it. Without judging anything.
Just notice what comes and goes in this moment of watching.

Mindful breakfast

Try to slow down your breakfast and be conscious of every bite.

Just take a small bite into your mouth and chew it 20 - 30 times before swallowing it.

Do not take the next bite until your mouth is completely empty.

This will ensure optimal digestion. Chewing stimulates all digestive processes and makes it easier for the body to absorb nutrients.

At the same time, this exercise slows down your eating habits and makes you more conscious of your breakfast.

4-7-8 breathing

Sit comfortably or stand upright.

Breathe in slowly through your nose and count to 4.
Then hold your breath and count to 7.
Now relax your jaw, open your mouth and breathe out slowly while you
Count 8.

Repeat this for several breathing cycles.

Record breakfast

When you have breakfast with your family or roommates, try not to mindlessly eat while getting lost in conversation.

Try to be the slowest person in the group to eat.

This way, you can relax and be mindful while eating, at least for a few moments.

A good start for more rest overall during the day.

Sensory breakfast

Arrange your breakfast in a way that pleases your eyes.
Look at your food mindfully and consciously before you start eating breakfast.
Pay attention to the colors, textures and arrangement of the foods on your plate.

Close your eyes briefly and concentrate on the scent.
Can you smell spices?
What does the scent remind you of?

Try to feel the food in your mouth while eating.
How does the consistency change while chewing?
What taste experiences are released?

Listen to the sounds that come with chewing.

Enjoyable drinking

Take time to consciously drink a last cup of tea or coffee before you start your day.

Focus on the temperature and taste in your mouth.

Can you feel the path of your drink after swallowing? Do you also feel the warmth in your throat and stomach? How does your drink taste on your tongue? Does the taste or smell remind you of a pleasant situation?

Sip your drink loudly and with enjoyment to enjoy it with concentration and mindfulness.

Reflection after breakfast

After breakfast, take a moment to mindfully reflect on your food.

How do you feel physically and emotionally after breakfast?

Are you full or still slightly hungry?
Does your body still want something sweet?
How does your body feel? Are you tired?
Did you enjoy the meal?

Feel into your body whether your food has made you full and satisfied.

View of the egg timer

Before the hustle and bustle of everyday life begins, take a little conscious time out to relax.

Set an egg timer for 1 minute.
Alternatively, you can also use your cell phone timer or an alarm clock.

Do nothing at all for 1 minute.

Try to sit completely still and not move your body or face.

Relaxation Mantra

After breakfast, sit at the table for a moment and combine your slow breathing through your nose with a small mental mantra to relax yourself internally.

As you inhale, mentally begin the sentence
"I am..."
and as you exhale you add
"... completely relaxed."

Or

"I go..."
-
"... start the day relaxed."

Feel free to repeat this mantra over and over again within 2-3 minutes.

STOP

STOP!
Take a moment after breakfast and stop whatever you
are doing.
Is the table still full of dishes?
Anyway, take a short break.

Look around!

How many things can you see in your environment
that are BLUE?

**Look in all directions and try to find 5 different blue
objects.**

Use this exercise to briefly arrive in the here and now
before you start your day.

30

WORK/ SCHOOL/ STUDY

This chapter introduces you to mindfulness exercises that you can easily integrate into your everyday work, school and university life.

Whether you are on your way to work, between meetings or taking a short break outside, the exercises presented invite you to consciously perceive the present.

The exercises in this chapter allow you to take advantage of the often overlooked moments of short walks and breaks to calm your mind while increasing your physical activity.

Discover a simple yet powerful way to incorporate mindfulness into your daily movements with the following mindfulness exercises.

Slow down your driving style

Are you by any chance traveling by car?
Try to use your way to work/university/school etc.
today for a mindfulness exercise:

**Drive in a relaxed manner on the road that is not intended for overtaking.
Try to stick to the recommended speed or even deliberately keep it 5 km/h below the maximum speed.**

Consciously slow down your driving style and drive as relaxed as possible.

How does it feel?

Can you notice a difference when you arrive?

Conscious arrival

Once you reach your destination, pause for a moment and become aware of your surroundings.

Breathe in and out deeply once.

Feel the air you breathe.
Is it cold? Is it warm?

Can you perceive certain sounds?

Do you notice certain smells?

Do you consciously notice an object today that you have never noticed before?

Pay conscious attention to things that you notice for the first time and only then continue on your way.

Screen pause

Have you been looking at a screen and working continuously for an extended period of time?

Give yourself and your eyes a break to relax.

Close your eyes and gently massage your eyelids with your index fingers.
Take 1 to 2 minutes to do this.

Now choose two objects.
An object at a distance of about one meter and another object as far away as possible.
Focus on an object for 1-2 seconds and then jump your focus to the next object.
Switch back and forth between distances about 10-20 times.

This helps to relax the muscles of the eyes.

Quiet relaxation

Before you move on to the next task or quickly run to the next lecture hall, take a short, mindful break.

Remain still for a moment, either standing or sitting.

Take this short time for yourself and focus your attention exclusively on your breathing and your body. Try not to think, not to speak, not to read and to block out noises.

Take a deep breath before moving on to the next task. Allow yourself short breaks like this throughout the day.

Sensory relaxation technique

You can do this exercise standing or sitting.
If you feel stressed or negative thoughts dominate you, try
Count down to 5.

Make this conscious by:

**5 Consciously perceive the things you see.
4 things you notice that you feel.
3 things you notice when you hear them.
2 notice things that you smell.
1 thing you notice, that you taste.**

During the exercise, pay conscious attention to your surroundings.
Do you suddenly notice things that you didn't notice before?
By concentrating on your surroundings you will become calmer and more relaxed.

Breath Focus

Whatever you are doing, stop and pause for a moment.

Take 10 deep breaths and consciously breathe in and out powerfully.

Gently push aside any thoughts that arise and just observe your breathing.
How does the breath flow through your throat into your lungs and out again?
Do you breathe more into your chest or stomach area?

Do not continue your activity until you have taken 10 deep breaths.

Positive Affirmations

Are you very stressed right now?
Then use a short break for an affirmation exercise.

Repeat silently or in your mind sentences such as
"I am calm and relaxed."
or
"I do my best and that is enough."

This helps calm the mind and activate positive energy.

You can also choose a longer mantra to repeat, such
as
*"I'm learning to take breaks. There's nothing wrong
with taking time out for yourself."*

Repeat your affirmations 10-15 times and try to feel
what is being said or thought.

Activate your body

Are you feeling tired and exhausted right now?
Then take a short time to consciously activate your
body again.

Stand with your legs wide apart.
Shake out your hands and arms.

**Now clench your hands into fists and tap lightly on
your chest and stomach.**
Try to increase the tempo of the gentle tapping and
get faster.
Tap your entire upper body from top to bottom and
back again.

Relax your hands and let your arms hang at your sides.

Feel into your upper body.
How do the areas you tapped feel?

Step-by-step mindfulness

Do you often travel short distances during the day, such as to a meeting room, the next classroom or lecture hall?

Use these brief opportunities to synchronize your breathing with your steps.

For example, breathe in for four steps and out for four steps:

Inhale - 1, 2, 3, 4 Exhale - 1, 2, 3, 4

This helps you stay present in the moment and gain new focus.

Walk steps consciously

If possible, choose the stairs instead of the elevator.

Walk up or down the stairs consciously, giving them your full attention.

Feel each step consciously.
Pay attention to how your weight shifts with each step.
Can you perceive tension and relaxation?

After you take the stairs, take a moment to take a few deep breaths and feel your legs.

How do they feel?

LUNCH BREAK

This chapter is dedicated to mindfulness exercises that you can specifically integrate into your lunch break.

The exercises in this chapter include exercises for conscious eating, stretching exercises and small energy boosters.

These exercises help you to fully enjoy the moment, release physical tension and increase your mental performance.

A conscious lunch break is an important part of the day to recharge your batteries, clear your mind and revitalize your body.

In the hustle and bustle of everyday life, we often forget to really relax and use the break as an opportunity to recover.

Feel how mindfulness during your lunch break helps you reduce stress and start the rest of the day with renewed energy.

Weather forecast

Use your lunch break to take a mindful walk outside. Be aware of nature and be fully aware of your surroundings.
Breathe in the fresh air deeply and then breathe it out again.

Then direct your attention to your inner "weather situation".

How would you describe your current mood in a weather forecast?
Is it stormy? Cloudy? Foggy? Rainy? Clear? Sunny?

Notice your current mood without further evaluating or describing it.

Take some more deep breaths and continue your walk.
The walk will help you clear your head and reduce stress hormones.

Short body scan

Use your lunch break to take a short walk.

As you walk, gradually direct your attention through your body and scan it.

Start with your toes and slowly work your way up.
Stay on each body region for about 10 to 20 seconds.

Pay attention to how different parts of your body feel.
Are they tense? Relaxed? Do you feel a tingling sensation? What temperature do they perceive?

Scan your entire body while walking.

42

Breath Energy Meditation

Sit down on a chair and make yourself comfortable.
Place your feet hip-width apart on the floor.
Place your hands relaxed in your lap and concentrate
on your breathing to calm down.

Focus your attention on your feet.

Imagine that your current energy level is in your feet.

Try to supply your body with more energy with each breath.

With each breath, charge another "energy bar",
starting with the feet and working your way up
through the knees, stomach, neck and head.
Once you reach your head, feel the new energy
throughout your body.

43

Mudra-Meditation

Sit upright on a chair.
Place your hands on your thighs.

Turn your palms upwards and touch the tips of your thumbs with the tips of your index fingers on both sides, with the remaining fingers spread apart.

Visualize yourself absorbing peacefulness and harmony through your fingertips and distributing and flowing it into the rest of your body.

Can you feel the tension leaving you and you becoming calm?

44

Stretching

Stand in a relaxed position.

**Stretch both arms towards the ceiling.
The fingertips point upwards.**

Make yourself as big and as long as possible.

**Hold this position for about 5 seconds and then let
your arms fall next to your upper body - exhale
audibly.**

Shake your arms and repeat
the process several times.

Thought focusing

Find a quiet place where you will not be disturbed. Sit up straight and close your eyes.

Feel the air flowing into your nose, lifting your chest and flowing out of your body again.
Just concentrate on your breathing.

While breathing, thoughts and sensations will arise. Allow these thoughts to come and go without clinging to them or judging them.
Don't try to influence them, just watch them like clouds passing by in the sky.

Gently bring your attention back to your breathing again and again.
Continue the exercise for about 5 minutes and then consciously return to your surroundings.

Eat slowly & enjoy

Take a little more time for your lunch today.
Plan at least 20 minutes for your meal.

Consciously put your cutlery aside after each bite.

Do not pick up the cutlery until your mouth is completely empty.

Then prepare the next bite calmly with your cutlery and then put the bite in your mouth.
Then put the cutlery aside again.

Give yourself a short break halfway through your meal.

Through this exercise, you automatically slow down your eating behavior and avoid gobbling down food quickly during your break.

47

Hunger-satiety perception

Do you eat together with colleagues during your lunch break?
Then try not to lose yourself in conversation, but give your hunger some attention every now and then.

While you eat, pay regular attention to your inner feelings and ask yourself the following questions:

**Am I still hungry?
Or do I already feel full?**

If you feel full, leave some of your meal aside.
You can eat more later if you feel hungry again.
After eating, sit back for a moment and take the time to consciously perceive the feeling of satiety.

Snacks

Before you open the bag of candy, stop for a moment and ask yourself:

Am I really hungry?
Or am I stressed? Bored? Sad?

Recognize and fulfill the actual need.

If you are not hungry, do something else, such as take a short walk or make yourself a strengthening tea.

Are you really hungry?
Then eat the snack consciously and slowly.
Notice how the snack tastes and how it reduces your hunger.

Conscious drinking

During your break, take the time to consciously enjoy a refreshing drink.

Pay attention to the smell, temperature and color of the drink.

Let the drink slowly slide over your tongue and taste the different flavors and nuances.
Notice how the drink feels in your mouth.
Does it cool the oral cavity or does it warm it?

Feel your throat opening as you swallow.

This exercise will help you make drinking a mindful and conscious act that allows you to fully experience and enjoy the moment.

FREE TIME ACTIVITIES

This chapter introduces you to the world of mindful leisure activities that you can easily integrate into your day.

Here you will learn exercises to clear your mind, let go of negative thoughts and focus on the present moment.

The presented mindfulness exercises in the area of leisure time are designed to offer alternatives to spending time in front of the television.
Whether you're out in nature or just taking a short break at home, these exercises will help calm your mind and change your perspective.

These mindfulness exercises can help reduce stress, promote creativity, and improve overall mental clarity.

Note method

Do you find it difficult to find an alternative to television or your cell phone when you're bored? Then try the note method:

Fill a jar with 26 pieces of paper on each of which you write a letter of the alphabet.

Whenever you feel bored on a given day, pull a piece of paper out of the jar.
Which letter is on the piece of paper? Decide spontaneously what comes to mind when you think of this letter.
Is it a cooking idea, a destination or a game?
You can also let the thoughts continue.

"P - Paella - Spain - Sun - Sunset"

Watch the sunset in a special place today.
What is important is not what you do, but that you do it quickly and do not postpone it.

Cloud fantasizing

Is the weather dry and the sky cloudy today?
Then grab your picnic blanket and head outside.

Lie down on your blanket in the garden or a park and look up at the sky.

Now consciously perceive the clouds that you can see.
What do the clouds look like?
Can you recognize objects or figures?

Watch the clouds as they pass by and change their shapes.
What do you think about this?

This exercise can also be done in pairs or with several people and you can share your impressions and stories with each other.

Tactful walking

Use your free time for a little exercise with music.

Go for a walk and use your headphones to play your favorite music.

Adjust your steps to the beat of the music.
How does your body perceive this harmony?

Change your running beat with the next song.
How does the new rhythm feel to you?

Observe how this rhythm affects your mood.
Does it make you happier, more balanced or more relaxed?

Activate both hemispheres of the brain

Stand upright and let your arms hang at your sides. Now swing your arms - with your right arm starting at the front and your left arm at the back.

While your arms swing in different directions, you start from
10 to count backwards to 0.
When you're done, try spelling your name (including your last name) backwards.

Try to concentrate only on your exercises.
Do you find it difficult or easy?

Activating both hemispheres of the brain results in the brain having better learning performance and memory functioning better.

Barefoot running

Our feet were not born for shoes - give them a little exercise today.

If the weather permits, use your free time and find a piece of meadow or soft forest floor.

Take off your shoes and socks and walk a few steps barefoot.

Consciously roll your feet slowly.
Feel the earth beneath your feet.
How does the ground feel?
Is it soft or hard?
Warm or cold?

Put all your attention into the soles of your feet.

Try to put all thoughts aside and just focus on the feeling of your feet.
This way you can experience nature even more intensely.

5 Finger Method

To do the exercise, go to a quiet place and take some
time to consciously think about the questions.
Look at the palm of your hand.
Each finger represents a different question
1 - Thumb:
Which of your strengths make you proud?
What talents do you particularly like about yourself?
2 - Index finger:
***Is there something in nature that inspires and excites
you?***
3 - Middle finger:
***Who would you like to do something good for today
and can you do something good for? And what can
you do for him/her?***
4 - Ring finger:
Which person is particularly dear to you?
What do you appreciate so much about him/her?
5 - Little finger:
What are you especially grateful for?
You can do this exercise whenever you want to
strengthen yourself mentally.

Taking photos

Take some time today for your creativity & your memory.
You don't need to have excellent photography skills to do this exercise, even your phone's camera will do.
This mindfulness practice is about viewing photography as a mirror of reality.

While you walk, take some photos.

After you have taken the pictures, look closely at the area you photographed.
In the evening, take these pictures and compare them with the impressions you have stored in your memory.

Did you perceive the surroundings as they are depicted in the picture?
Focus again on the impressions you have made.

On a discovery tour

Find an object, preferably from nature, such as a leaf, a blade of grass or a stone.

Now consider this subject carefully.

Examine it from all sides, hold it up to the light, look at it from close up and from a distance.

What structures on the surface do you notice? Do you notice small patterns?
Pay attention to dots, lines, colors and bumps. What is the texture of your object?
Does it feel hard, soft or smooth?

Take a few minutes to consciously discover and marvel at the small world of this object.

Gardening

Do you have a garden or a balcony?
Then give your full attention to gardening today.

Feel the movements of your hands as you plant new seeds.
Consciously remove a little soil and feel its consistency in your hands.
Is it wet or dry?
Clayey or sandy?

Take a seed in your hand that you want to plant.
Realize the great feat this little seed accomplishes until it becomes a big plant.

Lose yourself completely in your task and focus only on planting to create a deeper connection with nature.

Wait!

Waiting as mindfulness training is an effective and long-term exercise.
Standing in line at the supermarket, in the doctor's waiting room or waiting at a red light:
When we wait, we are often annoyed because we perceive waiting as wasted time.

Use the waiting times consciously just for yourself and take time for a mindfulness exercise.
Breathe in deeply and breathe out deeply.
Observe your breath flowing in and out through your nose.
Tell yourself mentally
"When I breathe in, I give myself peace and when I breathe out, I feel relaxed."

If you do something useful while you are waiting, the waiting will be
more bearable and you become more relaxed.

HOUSEHOLD TASKS

This chapter is dedicated to the art of practicing mindfulness even in everyday moments such as household chores.

Here you will find practical exercises that you can integrate while tidying up or cleaning to create short moments of reflection and calm.

The purpose of cleaning is to remove the dirt from the mind and purify our hearts. Cleaning is a practice to focus on the present. When cleaning, you don't think about anything unnecessary and you concentrate fully on the work.

The practices range from consciously feeling the water to movement exercises.

These mindful moments can not only reduce stress, but also help increase energy and clarity for the rest of the day.

Feeling water

Are you still busy doing the dishes and your
thoughts are already on your next to-dos?
Use the time to be a little more mindful.

**When you come into contact with the water, be
aware of it and sharpen your sense of touch.**

How does the water feel on your skin?
Is it rather hard or do you find it soft?

Rub your hands together.
Do you feel the dishwashing liquid on your skin?
Does it leave a light film or foam?

This is how you train the mindfulness of your senses.

Vibrations-Meditation

You can do this meditation while cleaning windows or vacuuming, for example.

Breathe in deeply through your nose and slowly out through your mouth and hum your absolute favorite song.
Hmmm, hmm, hmm, hmm.

Allow the vibration to travel and spread through the body - from the oral cavity to the forehead, chest, back and stomach.
Focus on how the sound feels, not how it sounds.

Repeat this several times to allow the vibration to spread.
How do the areas of your body feel where you feel the vibration?

Declutter

The dark side of consumption:
We accumulate too much and value it too little.
It's time to change that!

Start by decluttering your apartment.

Anything you haven't used in a year can go.
Things that you rarely use and that are not very
important to you should also be sorted out.
Instead of throwing them away, donate them and
make someone else happy.

By decluttering regularly, you not only create order
in your home, but also in your mind.
You don't have to do everything at once. Take 15
minutes a day to sort out a drawer or look through a
shelf.

Breathe & Clean Up

Connect your breathing and cleaning:
Use your breath to clear clutter.

Inhale - pick up object,
Exhale - put the object back in its correct place.

Pay attention to this breathing until you finish cleaning.

This technique helps you stay in a calm and focused state.

Ritualization of cleaning

Consider cleaning as a ritual act and create a pleasant atmosphere around you.
Play soothing music, light a candle or use essential oils to create a relaxing mood.

Close your eyes every now and then and focus exclusively on the scent.

Does the scent become more intense?
Does the scent remind you of something?
How does the scent affect your feelings?
Does your body react in any way to the scent?

Try not to judge, just feel.

Use the short break to focus and recharge your batteries. Then continue with your household tasks.

Dancing vacuuming

Use the vacuum cleaner for a little dance session.
Turn on your favorite music and let it sink in for a while.
Now start moving loosely.
Shake your arms, bounce your legs, circle your hips, nod your head - just do whatever feels good.
Let your body dance on its own, according to how it feels.

Try to shake off the stresses of the day with every movement.

Also use strong exhalations to enhance the release of stress.

After you've shaken everything off, give yourself some time to enjoy the music and clear your mind.

Slowly & thoroughly

Be slow and thorough when cleaning.
Clean each surface carefully and perform each movement consciously.

Practice mindful action by performing each action with full attention.

Be conscious when you take the rag, for example, dip it in the water and then clean the area. Focus on making each movement with precision and calmness.

Feel free to try doing everything more slowly than usual.
How does it feel to you?

Walking around blind

Do you know your apartment inside and out?
Then check how well you know your home while you're cleaning:

Close your eyes and walk through the rooms.
Try walking around "blind" for about two minutes.

If this is too easy for you, try doing everyday tasks like cleaning.

This helps you to become more aware of your familiar surroundings and to sharpen your senses.
You will also experience the activities you perform in a different way.

Spin cycle

Do you have to wait another 3 minutes until the washing machine is finished and you can empty it? Use the time for a little exercise:

Stand with your legs wide apart and your knees slightly bent.
Begin to gently rock by bending and straightening your legs.
Rock about 130 to 140 times per minute, leaving all other parts of your body relaxed so they can swing along to the rhythm.

Imitate the spin cycle of your washing machine.

You can also relax your neck and let your head tilt towards your chest.

Shake off all the stresses of the day so far.

Conscious termination

Have you finished your household chores for today?
Then consciously finish cleaning or tidying up.

Take a moment to look at your clean home and
appreciate your efforts.

Breathe deeply.
Can you smell the cleanliness?

**Feel inside yourself.
Enjoy the feeling of satisfaction after your work is
done.**

DINNER

This chapter invites you to take mindful breaks during your dinner – whether alone or with your family or friends.

Here you will find targeted exercises to help you feel gratitude, to consciously perceive your food, to consciously calm down, to clear your mind and to gain new energy.

The practices range from awareness exercises to mindful eating that can be perfectly incorporated into a dinner meal.

These mindful breaks allow you to reduce stress, increase concentration and create a positive atmosphere for the rest of the day.

Mindful listening

Are you having company at dinner?
Then try to be a good listener today.
Mindful communication requires not only keeping an
eye on your own needs, but also considering the
needs of the person you are communicating with.
This means being aware of the context or
environment in which the conversation partner finds
himself, be it within a family, a circle of friends or
another situation.

**So today, just try to listen to the other person
compassionately - without interrupting or wanting
to react or answer straight away.**

How does it feel to you?
How does it feel for your conversation partner?

Tangerines

Try to eat a tangerine for dinner today, mindfully and with focus.

Carefully take the tangerine in your hand and look at it closely.

Pay attention to their shape, color and the structure of their shell.
Smell it and enjoy the wonderful, fresh citrus scent.
Then slowly start peeling the tangerine and notice what is hidden under the skin. When you separate the individual pieces and eat them, pay attention to what you taste.
Be attentive and feel how the sweet juice plays around your tongue and what sensations arise.
"What's the point of eating a tangerine?
The point is simply to eat them.
The moment you eat a tangerine, that act is the most important thing in your life."
-Thich Nhat Hanh-

Cherry exercise

Get into a position where you are aware of your breathing. Pause for a moment and re-center yourself.

Now take a raisin in your hand and look at it carefully, as if it were completely new to you.
Pay attention to their texture, color and how the light falls on them.
Explore their smell and the sounds they make when you crush them.
Put the raisin in your mouth, resist the temptation to eat it right away, and let it roll on your tongue and the insides of your cheeks.
Feel its texture and how it feels.
Bite gently on the raisin and concentrate on its intense flavor as you continue to move it in your mouth.
Start chewing slowly, paying attention to the development of flavor and the disintegration of the raisin. Take a sip of water to accompany the dissolving sensation of the raisin.

3 beautiful experiences

Do you eat dinner with your family or friends?
Then use the time together to talk about your best
experiences of the day.

**Take a little time and tell each other the three best
things you experienced that day.**
Why are you grateful for this?
What feelings do these three things evoke in you?

By focusing your attention on the little things, you
will be able to consciously focus on the positive
aspects of life.

It also strengthens the bond, sharing beautiful
experiences with each other and is a nice way to
end the day.

Focused eating

Find a quiet place to eat and sit down at a table.

Put your smartphone aside and focus on your meal.

Avoid standing, walking, working or watching television while eating as these are distracting and should be avoided.

Instead, concentrate on the food in front of you and give it your full attention.
Consciously take a short break before meals.

Before you pick up your knife and fork, take three deep breaths.
Leave the stress of the day behind you and try to relax.

Do these breaths as a ritual before every mindful meal.

Favorite people

After eating, take a moment to reflect.

What people come to mind who were kind or helpful today, last week, a long time ago or when you were younger?

Try to get to 5 people.
What memories do you have of them and the situations?

Remember the people on your life path so far and feel gratitude.

Silent meal

Begin your meal in silence.

Today, try not to talk while you eat and instead focus on consciously enjoying each bite.
Even if you are in company, just do the test together.

Don't pay attention to your surroundings, just pay attention to your meal.
Enjoy every bite and the taste.
Forget the world around you.

How did it feel for you?
How did it feel to be silent and enjoy your company?

The Silent Meal is a simple but powerful practice that can help you create a deeper connection with your food and your body.

Off to the corner

Are you worried or angry right now?
Before you start your meal, sit or stand in a relaxed position.
Close your eyes and take a deep breath.

Let your thoughts run free.

When negative thoughts arise, try to mindfully "put them in the corner".
Take your worries or your anger, place them in the corner of the room with the help of your thoughts and consciously turn away or leave the room.

Additionally, check the following:
Will these things still interest you in 5 years?
If not, don't give them more than 5 minutes of your current thoughts!

Alone in a restaurant

For many people, sitting alone in a restaurant is a challenge.
However, it can be a nice way to become more aware of your surroundings.

Who are the people in the restaurant with you?

Try to find the 5 happiest people in the room, in your opinion.
Now be aware of what you are basing your choice on.
Are they facial expressions or body postures?

Think about what could make the people happy right now.

Are you perhaps one of the 5 people?
What makes you happy right now?

Gratitude

Before you start your meal:
Sit comfortably at the table and place your hands
quietly on the table or on your lap.

Look at your food carefully.

Think for a moment about all the steps and people it
took to get this food to you – the farmers who grew
the vegetables, the people who harvested,
transported and prepared them.
Be aware of how much effort and care went into each
ingredient.

**Take a moment to express your gratitude internally
or out loud.**

You can say something like:
*"I am grateful for this meal and for everyone who
helped bring it before me."*

RECREATION

This chapter is about creating a relaxed environment for yourself and taking some targeted me-time.

Consciously take time for yourself!
Choose a time of the week when you do something good for yourself and consciously designate it as me-time.

Here you will find targeted exercises for a relaxing bath, a digital detox or simply for consciously doing nothing.

You decide how you want to spend your me-time.

This promotes self-love and helps you become more relaxed.
Also mark the appointment in your calendar so you don't miss it.

Digital Detox

Today is time for digital detox.

Try to spend an hour or the whole evening offline today.

No distractions from your phone, TV or tablet.

How do you feel about it?
Do you feel bored?
Then find other mindfulness exercises from this book to pass the time.

If you notice that the offline break is good for you, then extend it further soon.
Maybe you can even manage a whole day!?

Relaxation bath

End your day with a relaxing bath in the tub and take the time to experience it consciously.

Feel the warm water enveloping your body.
Do you notice differences in the sensitivity of different areas of the skin?
Does the heat feel more intense in some parts of your body than in others?

Lather your body vigorously from head to toe.
Feel how your skin reacts to the application of shower gel or soap.
Do certain parts of the body cool down quickly?

Try to put distracting thoughts aside and fully enjoy the bathing experience.

82

Do nothing!

Find a place where you can lie down, sit or stand comfortably. Close your eyes and allow yourself to be completely still for a brief moment.

Take 5 minutes and consciously do NOTHING. No distractions.
You don't have to pay attention to anything.
Just do nothing.

Let your mind rest, without distraction or pressure.

Feel the silence around you and the silence within you. Notice what it feels like to do nothing, without expectations or goals.
Allow yourself to simply be there, without doing or thinking anything. This moment of conscious doing nothing can help you to take yourself out of the hectic routine of everyday life and to be more conscious of the here and now.

Accept and forgive mistakes

Forgiving yourself is a big part of mindfulness.
This allows you to come to terms with your past and
begin to live in the here and now.

**Write down on a piece of paper which mistakes from
the past bother you and which characteristics you
don't like about yourself.**

Throw these pieces of paper into a box one by one
and say out loud or in your mind

"I forgive myself."

Think about what you would do differently or better
in the future.
Let go of the past and focus on the present.

Favourite Song

You can do this meditation in your retreat or in any other undisturbed place.
Sit up straight, close your eyes and breathe in and out calmly.

Put on headphones or play your favorite song loudly.

Focus on your feelings while doing this.
What does this song trigger in you?
Does it make you happy?
Does it trigger a memory of a specific event?

You can not only limit this mindfulness exercise to a specific song, but you can do it with your entire playlist.
This not only increases your awareness of listening, but also creates space to engage with your feelings.

Everyone needs an oooohm!

Sit upright and focus your attention on the silence around you.

Breathe in deeply through your nose.
As you exhale, open your mouth and make the sound "Ooooo", then close your mouth again for the "hmmmm".

"Oooooooohmmm"

Try to hold the sound as long as possible.

Feel the vibration flowing from your head into your chest.

Repeat this process several times for 2-3 minutes to feel the vibration throughout your body.

Emotional painting

Sit down at a table and lay out a large piece of paper in front of you (at least A3). It is best to fix it with weights.
Grab a pen - preferably a soft pencil or a colored pencil.

Now close your eyes and paint your mood.
Follow your inner feelings and impulses.

Do you prefer to paint soft, wide circles?
Or do you want to paint hard edges and zigzag patterns when you are angry and tense?

Just focus on the movement and not on what the image might look like.
Paint for as long as feels right.
Then look at your picture.
Can you recognize your feelings?
Repeat the exercise on another day and compare the results.

Foot massage

Sit cross-legged.
If you are still wearing socks, take them off.

Take your right foot in your hands and massage it vigorously.
Pay attention to the top of your foot, as well as your heel and the sole of your foot.

Count slowly to 20.

When the time is up, stop the massage and feel into your foot.
Does it feel different than your left foot?

Then massage your left foot for 20 seconds.
Do both feet feel the same again afterwards?

Light Meditation

Assume a relaxed position on the floor or on a chair.

Place a candle or tea light about one meter in front of you and light it.

Relax and focus your gaze on the flickering of the fire.
Observe whether the flame changes in color and shape and whether you can hear any faint sounds of the fire.
Try to switch off your thoughts while doing this.
If thoughts arise, gently push them aside and focus on the light again.

Enjoy this peace and let it work on you for a moment.

Hand on heart

Find a comfortable and relaxed position, either sitting or lying down, and gently close your eyes.

Place your right hand on your heart and your left hand on your stomach.

Focus your full attention on the feeling in your hands.

Feel the warmth flowing from your hands into your chest and stomach.

Can you feel the slight pressure your hands apply to these areas?

Relax completely and enjoy the touch and the slow spread of warmth throughout your body.

Take 3 to 5 minutes to do this exercise to calm down and relax.

GOOD NIGHT!

This chapter invites you to end the day in a relaxed manner.

Here you will find mindfulness exercises that you can do before going to bed to create a harmonious transition from the end of your day to sleep.

The exercises range from short meditations to relaxation exercises that can easily be done in bed or on the sofa.

These mindful moments not only help calm the mind, but also create space for reflection and gratitude.

This chapter allows you to shake off the events of the day and enter into a relaxed sleep.

Body scan

Are you ready to end the day and are you looking for some final relaxation before going to sleep?
Then this is the perfect time for a body scan.

Lie down in your bed.

Feel your back resting on the mattress.
Which parts of your body do you touch the surface with?
With your shoulders? Your arms? Your bottom? Or your heels?

Scan your body from head to toe and briefly feel all parts of your body.
How do the body parts feel?
Are you tense?

Try to continue to relax.
When you have finished the body scan, you can breathe in and out deeply a few more times, continue to calm down and try to fall asleep.

91

Gratitude

Remember again the events and experiences of today that were positive and beautiful for you.

Imagine it again in your mind's eye.
Think also of the "little" things that we often take for granted, like the warm rays of sunshine, the smell of coffee in the morning, the smile of the cashier...

Try to find 5 positive & beautiful events.
Summarize these moments in words to make them even more memorable.

"The delicious coffee in the morning made me feel refreshed and awake, so I could start the day motivated."

This way you focus on the positive things and feel gratitude.

Sunbathing

Lie down on your bed or sofa.

Now rub both your hands together firmly.

Do this until they are completely warm.
Now place it directly on your stomach without any clothes in between.

Imagine a warm ray of sunshine flowing from your hands into your stomach.
With every breath the light becomes brighter and warmer.

Feel into your stomach.
Does it feel warm?

Imagine the sun shining into your belly and warming you from the inside.

Counting to sleep

Prepare to go to bed and find a comfortable sleeping position that makes you feel comfortable.

To make it easier to fall asleep, focus on letting go of your thoughts by counting your breaths and repeating a calming mantra.

Start counting by
Inhale - think "1" and as you exhale think "I am falling asleep."
Continue with the
Inhale - "2" & Exhale "I'm falling asleep."

Repeat this process until you are able to fall asleep.
If thoughts interrupt you, gently push them aside and start again.
Have a restful night!

Dream Trip

Lie down relaxed on your sofa or bed.
Close your eyes and try to breathe calmly and
relaxed.
Release your jaw muscles and tongue from the roof
of your mouth.

**Now travel with your thoughts to a beautiful
meadow of flowers.**

Hear the bees buzzing.
Feel the grass tickling beneath your feet.
Hear the wind blowing through the trees.
Feel the sun on your skin.

Enjoy your dream trip and try to stay in this place
for a while and enjoy the peace and quiet.

95

Show tiredness

Use the evening hours to show your tiredness and yawn really loudly.
Even if you have to help yourself yawn.

To do this, breathe in deeply, open your mouth, lift your soft palate and make yawning noises.

Try yawning loudly 10-20 times.

Yawning relaxes the throat, palate, upper neck and base of the brain.
It also has a mood-balancing effect.
It calms you down when you're nervous and cheers you up when you're down.

A great exercise to prepare you for sleep.

Shed ballast

Sit or lie down in a relaxed position.
Breathe in and out calmly.

Try to let go of something from this day and shed ballast.

What do you choose?
A conversation that made you angry?
An other opinion?
A saying that hurt you?
A worry that you carry within you?

Get rid of anything that is weighing you down mentally so you don't carry it with you into the next day.
Concentrate on this ballast and consciously breathe it out and blow it away with force.

Take a few breaths to do this.

97

Positive Affirmation

Use the last minutes of your day for positive affirmations.

Repeat positive sentences quietly or in your mind, such as

"I am grateful for the day and can relax and unwind."

or

"I am happy and satisfied and look forward to tomorrow."

Feel free to repeat the sentences 10 - 20 times or replace them with another affirmation after a few repetitions.

98

Pillow breathing

Lie down in a position that feels comfortable.
Close your eyes and breathe relaxed.

Place a pillow on your stomach and then relax your arms next to your body.
Now concentrate on your breathing.

Can you feel the pillow rising as you inhale and falling as you exhale?

Now try to breathe more deeply into your stomach without letting the pillow fall down.

Consciously take deep breaths and then breathe out strongly.

Repeat this for 2-3 minutes.

End of day

Sit or lie down in a relaxed position.

Close your eyes and let a blank screen appear in your mind's eye.

Think back to the past few hours and review your day.
Which image appears before your eyes first?
Take another close look at your day.

Assume the attitude of a spectator and try to concentrate only on the images you see.

Try not to judge them any further and mentally close thc day.

Did you like this book?

Find more here
100 small & efficient exercises for everyday work:

imprint